Good Question!

How Does a Seed Sprout?
AND OTHER QUESTIONS ABOUT . . .
Plants

STERLING CHILDREN'S BOOKS
New York

STERLING CHILDREN'S BOOKS
New York

An Imprint of Sterling Publishing
387 Park Avenue South
New York, NY 10016

Text © by 2014 Melissa Stewart
Illustrations © by 2014 Sterling Publishing Co., Inc.

Photo credits: Getty Images © Gay Bumgarner: 5; iStockphoto.com © Ken Babione: 28; © flytosky11: 3, 9, 13, 17, 21, 26, 29, 30
(background); © Pauline S Mills: 20; © sierrarat: 28; Minden Pictures © Cyril Ruoso/JH Editorial: 22; Shutterstock.com
© Christopher Elwell: 4, 7, 8, 14, 17, 21, 23, 29 (caption plate); © IbagjaUsap: 20; © Bogdan Wankowicz: 8

ISBN 978-1-4549-0670-4 (hardcover)
ISBN 978-1-4549-0671-1 (paperback)

Library of Congress Cataloging-in-Publication Data

Stewart, Melissa.
How does a seed sprout? : and other questions about plants / Melissa Stewart.
  p. cm. -- (Good question)
Includes bibliographical references and index.
ISBN 978-1-4549-0670-4 (hardcover) -- ISBN 978-1-4549-0671-1 (pbk.) 1. Seeds--Juvenile
literature. 2. Plants--Juvenile literature. I. Title. II. Series: Good question!
QK661.S743 2014
635'.6--dc23

2013014429

Distributed in Canada by Sterling Publishing
c/o Canadian Manda Group, 165 Dufferin Street
Toronto, Ontario, Canada M6K 3H6
Distributed in the United Kingdom by GMC Distribution Services
Castle Place, 166 High Street, Lewes, East Sussex, England BN7 1XU
Distributed in Australia by Capricorn Link (Australia) Pty. Ltd.
P.O. Box 704, Windsor, NSW 2756, Australia

Design by Elizabeth Phillips and Andrea Miller
Art by Carol Schwartz

For information about custom editions, special sales, and premium and corporate purchases, please contact
Sterling Special Sales at 800-805-5489 or specialsales@sterlingpublishing.com.

Manufactured in China
Lot #:
2 4 6 8 10 9 7 5 3 1
10/13
www.sterlingpublishing.com/kids

CONTENTS

What is a plant?

Grass is a plant. So is a maple tree. Grape vines, rose bushes, and ferns are plants, too. Plants come in many different sizes and shapes. They grow in parks and gardens, fields and forests, and even in the ocean. Scientists have named more than 275,000 kinds, or species, of plants on Earth, and many more haven't been discovered yet.

How are plants different from animals? Most plants have three main parts—leaves, stems, and roots. Plants can grow up, or they can spread out, but they can't move from place to place. Most important of all, plants use sunlight to make their own food.

Animals couldn't live without plants. And that includes you! All the fruits and vegetables you eat come from plants. Bread, cereal, peanut butter, and chocolate chip cookies are made from plants, too. Almost all the foods you eat come from plants or animals that eat plants!

Some animals make their homes in, on, or under plants. And many people live in houses made of wood from trees. You breathe oxygen, a gas that plants give off. Other animals need oxygen, too.

This robust vegetable garden is full of a variety of plants.

What is a seed?

A pea is a seed. So is an acorn and a kidney bean and a grain of rice. Orchid seeds are so small you'd need a microscope to see them. Giant coco de mer palm seeds can weigh as much as an eight-year-old child. Wow!

Big or small. Round or flat. Smooth or rough or hairy. Every seed on Earth is the beginning of a plant. Most seeds also contain food for the developing plant. The seed and its food supply are wrapped inside a hard seed coat.

Do all seeds grow into new plants?

Cut an apple in half and count the seeds inside. Some apple trees can produce 200 apples a year. How many seeds would that be?

An oak tree can drop 100,000 acorns in one year. And a birch tree can produce 15 million seeds in one season. Just imagine what would happen if all those seeds grew into new trees!

Plants make lots and lots of seeds, but most of them never sprout. Many are eaten or crushed. Some rot. Others land in places where they can't take root.

Even seeds that sprout may not grow into strong, healthy plants. An apple tree may make 1,000 seeds a year, and an oak tree may drop 100,000 acorns. But only a few of those seeds develop into trees that make seeds of their own.

This squirrel munches on an acorn—a seed made by an oak tree.

This image shows six stages of a bean sprouting from a seed into a young plant.

How does a seed sprout?

For a seed to sprout, it must land in or on soil. But that's not the only thing a seed needs. Believe it or not, most seeds are pretty picky. The soil can't be too warm or too cold. It can't be too wet or too dry. And it has to have the perfect blend of minerals to help the plant grow.

Most seeds don't sprout right away. Many rest for a few months. Others wait a few years. And some seeds take much, much longer. What's the big holdup? They're waiting for their seed coats to break open.

Many seed coats soften when rain soaks them. Then, as sunlight warms the land, the seed coats dry out and crack open. Some seed coats will break open only after a fire burns the forest they live in.

Which part of a plant grows first?

As soon as a seed coat splits, a tiny root pushes out into the soil. It slides down through the dirt and begins to absorb, or take in, water and minerals.

Next, a slender shoot stretches up and pokes out of the soil. See how the plant's first tiny leaves slowly spread open? They stretch wide and start soaking up sunlight. Now the little plant can make all the food it needs to keep on growing.

Do all plants make seeds?

Nope. The first seed-making plants lived on Earth about 360 million years ago. But some kinds of plants have been around much longer. Some plants can trace their beginnings back 450 million years. How do they make new plants? They use tiny structures called spores instead of seeds.

You've probably seen mosses. They're small, soft plants with just one stem. That stem is covered with many leaves. Mosses grow in clumps in moist, shady places.

When the time is right, a tall, thin structure called a seta grows up, up out of most moss plants. At the top of the seta is a large capsule full of spores. When the seta reaches its full height, the capsule splits open. Hundreds, thousands, even millions of spores burst into the air. Some of them land in rich, damp soil and grow into a new moss plant.

Ferns make spores, too. If you turn over a fern leaf, or frond, and look at the bottom, you'll see dozens of tiny brown circles called sori. Each sorus is a cluster of tiny sacs, and each sac contains many, many spores. When the sacs break open, spores burst out and float on the wind. A few of the spores will grow into new fern plants, but most land in places where they can't sprout.

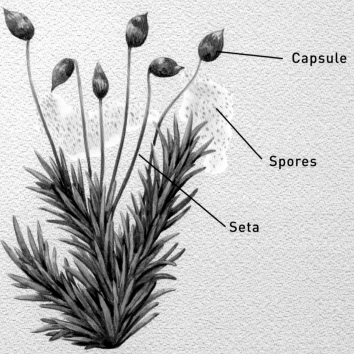

Capsule

Spores

Seta

Sorus

OXYGEN

LIGHT

CARBON DIOXIDE

WATER

WATER

How do leaves help a plant survive?

In most plants, leaves have a very important job to do. They use three ingredients—light, water, and a gas called carbon dioxide—to make food for the entire plant.

Carbon dioxide is in the air all around us. Plants breathe it in through tiny holes in their leaves. A plant's roots soak up rainwater, and tubes carry it up a plant's central stem to its leaves.

As rays of sunshine strike a leaf, a green material called chlorophyll collects light energy. That energy breaks apart the water and carbon dioxide inside a leaf. Then the plant uses some of those parts to build a sugary food called glucose. This process is called photosynthesis.

Why do leaves come in so many sizes and shapes?

You can tell a lot about a plant by looking at its leaves.

Why do wildflowers that grow in shady places have large, wide leaves? So they can soak up enough sunlight. A maple tree loses its leaves every autumn. It needs big leaves to collect a year's worth of energy in just a few months. A pine tree keeps its leaves all year long. It needs short, thin needles that won't get weighed down by snow.

No matter where a plant lives, its leaves are just the right size and shape to help it survive.

Why do plants need stems?

A plant's stems give it support. Small plants have soft, green stems. Trees have a trunk—a strong central stem made of wood. A tree's branches are made of wood, too.

Stems also transport food, water, and minerals. Water and minerals travel up from the roots to the leaves. At the same time, stems carry sugary food from the leaves to the rest of the plant.

Why are the stems of trees covered with bark?

A tree's bark is a lot like your fingernails. Your strong, stiff nails protect your fingertips. Bark protects the tender inside layers of a tree.

Take a close look at one of your fingernails. The part you can see and touch is dead. The living, growing part is hidden below the skin at the bottom of your nail.

The same is true for bark. The hard, outer layer you can see and touch is dead. But the layer underneath is still alive. As it grows, the tree becomes thicker.

All plants have a central stem as well as many smaller stems. A trunk is a tree's central stem. Branches are a tree's smaller stems.

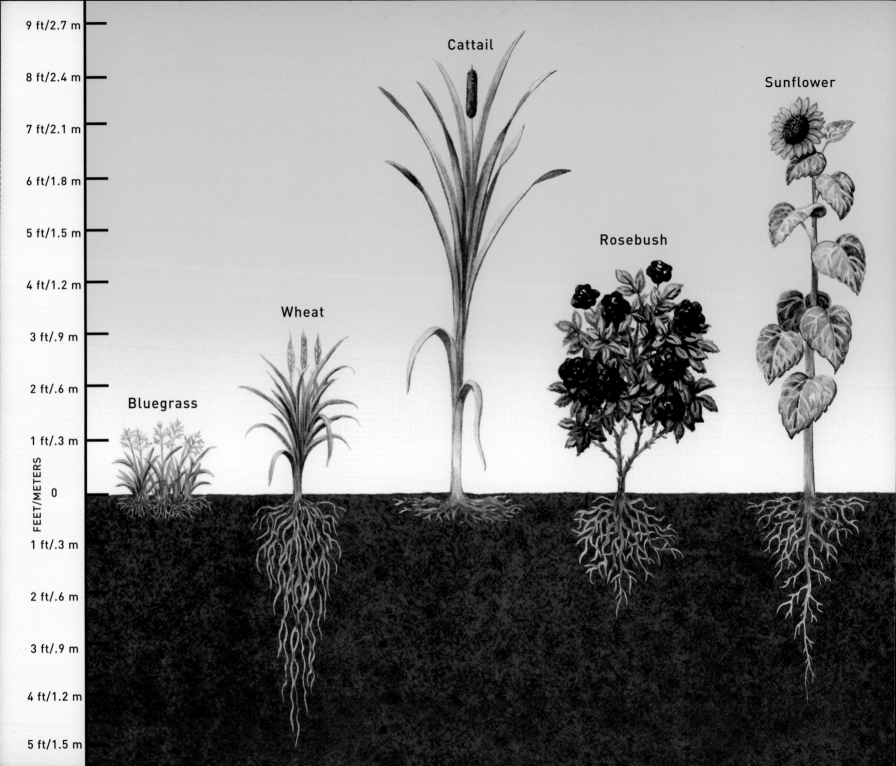

9 ft/2.7 m

8 ft/2.4 m

7 ft/2.1 m

6 ft/1.8 m

5 ft/1.5 m

4 ft/1.2 m

3 ft/.9 m

2 ft/.6 m

1 ft/.3 m

FEET/METERS

0

1 ft/.3 m

2 ft/.6 m

3 ft/.9 m

4 ft/1.2 m

5 ft/1.5 m

Cattail

Sunflower

Rosebush

Wheat

Bluegrass

How do roots help a plant survive?

Roots hold a plant in place and absorb water from the soil. Some plants have roots that grow down deep into the ground. Other plants have shallow roots that sprawl out in every direction.

Mosses don't have roots, but they do have tiny threads that anchor them to the soil. How are these threads different from the roots of ferns and seed-making plants? Moss threads can't absorb water. A moss plant gets its moisture from the air. And that means mosses have to live in places where the air is always damp. Most mosses grow in shady woodlands or wetlands.

Plants with roots can live almost anywhere, including hot, dry deserts. Desert plants may have root systems that are bigger than the network of stems and leaves we see above the ground. All those roots suck up the water desert plants need to carry out photosynthesis.

Roots also have another important job. They absorb minerals, such as calcium and iron. These minerals help plants grow big and strong. They also help plants fight off diseases. And when you eat those plants, they keep you strong and healthy, too.

A plant's roots lie below the soil. They help a plant absorb water and minerals. They also hold a plant in place so that it doesn't topple over.

What is a plant's secret weapon?

Flowers are a plant's secret weapon. A flower's bright, beautiful colors and sweet scent attract birds, bees, butterflies, and other animals. Why are they so interested in flowers? Because they're always on the lookout for a sweet treat.

A bee, for instance, knows that it can find a sugary juice called nectar deep inside a flower. As it feeds on nectar, a powdery material called pollen sticks to its body. Then the bee does the plant a really big favor—without even knowing it.

Plants can't move, so they need messengers to carry their pollen from one plant to another. This process is called pollination. As a bee moves from flower to flower in search of nectar, pollen goes along for the ride.

When pollen from one flower falls off the bee and lands on a different flower, a tiny tube opens up inside the flower. The pollen tumbles down the tube and lands in an area called the ovary. When material inside the pollen mixes with material inside a tiny ovule, a new seed starts to form. Many plants can't make seeds unless animals spread their pollen.

Pollen tube

Petal

Ovary

Ovule

Nectar

Which animals spread plant pollen?

As bees collect nectar to make honey, they pollinate 80 percent of all the flowering plants farmers grow in the United States. These plants include almonds, apples, beets, broccoli, cabbage, carrots, cauliflower, cherries, coconuts, cucumbers, grapes, green beans, kiwi, lemons, limes, melons, mustard, onions, pears, peas, peppers, squash, strawberries, and more. Bees also pollinate cotton plants. The white, puffy fruit of cotton is used to make clothes, bed sheets, and towels.

Butterflies, moths, and hummingbirds pollinate many of the plants people grow in flower gardens. Avocados, bananas, dates, figs, mangoes, and peaches all depend on bats to spread their pollen. Cocoa, the plant used to make chocolate, is pollinated by tiny flies called midges.

How do animals protect plants?

Some animals help plants by pollinating them. Others help plants by protecting them from plant-eating pests. Ladybugs come to the rescue by chowing down on aphids—tiny insects that harm plants by drinking their juices. Praying mantises feast on plant-destroying pests like fruit flies, beetles, and crickets.

Birds can help trees by eating insects that harm plants. This willow warbler carries a meal of caterpillars and insects to its chick.

Many birds and bats also protect plants. Grosbeaks, scarlet tanagers, and many kinds of warblers dine on caterpillar pests. Woodpeckers can hear insects inside trees and dig them out. Bats gorge on insects that destroy corn, soybeans, cucumbers, cotton, and pecans.

Why do some flowers smell bad?

Flowers come in all sizes, shapes, and colors—and smells! How a flower looks and smells is closely linked to how it's pollinated. Bright colors attract birds, bees, and butterflies. But bats fly at night. Most of the flowers they pollinate are white.

A plant named the Rafflesia arnoldii makes the largest flowers in the world. But they aren't very pretty. And, boy, do they stink! They smell like rotting meat. The nasty scent might make us feel sick, but the flies and beetles that spread the plant's pollen love the stench.

Wheat, rye, ragweed, corn, and other grasses are pollinated by the wind. Since these plants don't need help from animals, you might not notice their flowers. The spike at the top of a wheat plant can contain as many as twenty tiny flowers. Have you ever seen the tassels on a corn plant? Believe it or not, that's where you'll find its flowers.

Some plants can pollinate themselves. In plants like tomatoes, sunflowers, and lima beans, the structure that makes pollen is just above the place where the pollen tube forms. When pollen falls onto the right spot, a pollen tube opens up, and soon, a new seed starts to develop.

This photo of two huge Rafflesia flowers was taken in Indonesia.

What happens to a flower after it's pollinated?

As soon as seeds start to form, a flower's petals dry out and wither away. The plant's ovary swells and becomes a fruit.

When you hear the word "fruit," you probably think of apples and oranges, peaches and cherries, but not all fruits are round, colorful, and sugary sweet. Radishes and cucumbers are fruits. So are peapods and green beans.

A fruit protects the seeds developing inside it. When the seeds are ready to enter the world, the fruit ripens.

Why do some fruits taste so good?

If a plant dropped all its seeds on the ground, it would have to fight with its "children" for water, minerals, and sunlight. That's why a fruit's most important job is to scatter seeds.

Sweet fruits attract all kinds of animals. When a bear eats blueberries, the seeds pass through its digestive system. By the time the bear poops out the seeds, it may be miles away from the parent plant.

The hooks on common burdock fruits snag in animal fur. Wherever the animal goes, the fruit goes, too. And when the hooks break, the seeds land in a new place. Coconuts are light enough to float, so they can drift across the sea. Fruits have all kinds of ways of spreading seeds.

Do all seed-making plants produce flowers and fruit?

Flowering plants have lived on Earth for about 140 million years. Before they developed, most of the world's plants grew seeds inside of cones. Many of those plants are long gone. They died out millions of years ago—just like the dinosaurs. But a few have managed to survive. They include pine trees, cedars, redwoods, and spruces.

Today's cone-producing plants make two kinds of cones—pollen cones and ovule cones. The cones look different from one another, and they do different jobs.

How do pine trees make seeds?

A pine tree's ovule cones are large and woody, but the pollen cones are small and soft. When pollen cones open, wind picks up the pollen inside the cones and carries it through the air. If some of the pollen falls onto an ovule cone, material inside the pollen mixes with material inside an ovule. Then a new seed starts to form.

As pine seeds grow, so does the cone they're in. When the seeds are fully grown, their cone breaks open. The seeds fall out, and the wind whisks them away to new places.

A Pine Tree's Life

OVULE CONE
Pollen lands on one of the ovules inside an ovule cone and material inside the pollen and the ovule mix together. A new seed starts to form.

POLLEN CONE
First, pollen cones open and pollen is carried through the air.

SEED
As the pine seeds grow, so does their cone. When the seeds are ready to enter the world, the cone opens up. The seeds fall out and the wind takes them away.

YOUNG PINE TREE
The seed becomes a young pine tree.

ADULT PINE TREE
Some adult pine trees are about 200 feet (61 meters) tall.

27

Do all plants lose their leaves in cold weather?

Conifers have green needle-like leaves all year long. That's why many people call them evergreens. Evergreens lose just a few leaves at a time, so they are never bare. Conifers aren't the only evergreen plants. Holly, most azaleas, and boxwood are evergreens, too. Many people grow these plants in their gardens because they have green leaves in the winter.

Deciduous plants lose all of their leaves for part of the year. The leaves fall off at the end of the growing season. In cool parts of the world, leaves drift to the ground each autumn. In warm parts of the world, deciduous plants have no leaves during the dry season.

Does a plant ever stop growing?

Most people stop growing when they're between 16 and 21 years old. But plants never stop. They may take a break during the chilly winter months. But when the weather warms up, they start growing again. Plants keep on growing for as long as they live. Many plants live less than a year. They sprout in the spring and die in autumn. Their seeds survive through the winter and burst to life when the days grow warm. Some trees can live hundreds of years. Scientists working in the American West have found bristlecone pine trees that are almost 5,000 years old. No matter how old these trees get, they continue to make seeds and release them into the world. Because without seeds to sprout, there would be no more plants.

Ancient bristlecone trees like this one can live for more than five thousand years!

A Flowering Plant's Life

1. New seeds contain all the parts of a plant, including leaves, stems, root parts, and a food supply.

2. If a seed lands in a spot with just the right conditions, a plant will start to grow.

3. As the roots grow down through the soil, sprouts grow up toward the sun.

4. The leaves open up to absorb the sunlight and begin to produce food through photosynthesis.

5. Plants use flowers to produce new seeds so that new plants can grow.

6. When pollen from one flower lands on another flower, a fruit begins to form. Seeds grow inside the fruit.

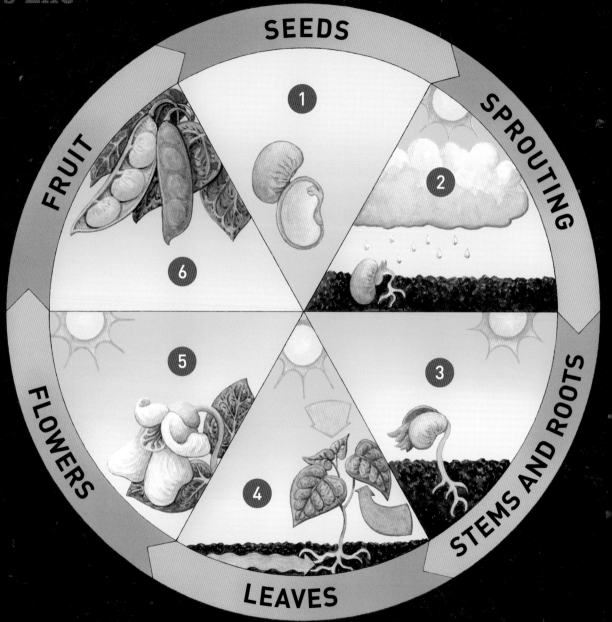

SEEDS

SPROUTING

STEMS AND ROOTS

LEAVES

FLOWERS

FRUIT

FIND OUT MORE

Books to Read

Aston, Dianna Hutts. *A Seed Is Sleepy*. San Francisco, CA: Chronicle Books, 2007.

Bang, Molly and Penny Chisholm. *Living Sunlight: How Plants Bring the Earth to Life*. New York: Blue Sky Press, 2009.

Dorros, Arthur. *A Tree Is Growing*. New York: Scholastic, 1997.

Galbraith, Kathryn O. *Planting the Wild Garden*. Atlanta: Peachtree Publishers, 2011.

Gibbons, Gail. *Tell Me, Tree: All About Trees for Kids*. New York: Little, Brown, 2002.

Kudlinski, Kathleen V. *What Do Roots Do?* Minnetonka, MN: Northword, 2005.

Stewart, Melissa. *How Do Plants Grow?* Tarrytown, NY: Benchmark Books, 2007.

Websites to Visit

FROM SEED TO PLANT
www.scholastic.com/teachers/lesson-plan/seed-plant

HOW PLANTS GROW
www.sciencekids.co.nz/gamesactivities/plantsgrow.html

PLANTS VIDEO
video.nationalgeographic.com/video/kids/green-kids/plants-kids

SEEDLING TIME LAPSE
www.neok12.com/php/watch.php?v=zX000e66
5066767b7b72457b&t=Plants

TIME LAPSE OF PLANTS GROWING
www.neok12.com/php/watch.php?v=zX651570
7a0f466267725159&t=Plants

TIME LAPSE OF RADISH SEEDS SPROUTING, ROOTS AND SHOOTS GROWING
www.neok12.com/php/watch.php?v=zX560a00
745f517353705577&t=Plants

INDEX